GOD'S LITTLE INSTRUCTION BOOK FOR THE CLASS OF 2015

GOD'S LITTLE INSTRUCTION BOOK FOR THE CLASS OF 2015

transforming lives together

GOD'S LITTLE INSTRUCTION BOOK FOR THE CLASS OF 2015
Published by David C Cook
4050 Lee Vance View
Colorado Springs, CO 80918 U.S.A.

David C Cook Distribution Canada
55 Woodslee Avenue, Paris, Ontario, Canada N3L 3E5

David C Cook U.K., Kingsway Communications
Eastbourne, East Sussex BN23 6NT, England

The graphic circle C logo is a registered trademark of David C Cook.

All rights reserved. Except for brief excerpts for review purposes, no part of this book may be reproduced or used in any form without written permission from the publisher.

Bible credits are located at the end of this book.

ISBN 978-0-7814-1249-0

© 2015 David C Cook

The Team: Ingrid Beck, Amy Konyndyk, Tiffany Thomas, Karen Athen
Cover Design: Nick Lee
Cover Photo: Shutterstock

Printed in the United States of America

First Edition 2015

1 2 3 4 5 6 7 8 9 10

121714

INTRODUCTION

Congratulations! As a member of the Class of 2015, you are part of a new and changing millennium filled with innovative technologies and amazing discoveries.

These exciting times have made the earth a much more challenging and complicated place to live. You will be confronted with opportunities to make wise decisions and to be a shining light in an often dark and confusing place. How do you make good choices when everything around you is moving and changing? And how do you cut through the hype and find what is good?

In *God's Little Instruction Book for the Class of 2015*, we offer you wisdom sufficient to help you navigate the twenty-first century. We have taken quotes from ordinary people and heroes throughout history and combined them with wisdom from the Bible to help you become the person you aspire to be. We hope the truths presented in these pages will help you settle your life on an unshakable foundation and enable you to build a world filled with infinite possibilities.

The world wants your best, but God wants your all.

—Author unknown

Thou shalt love the Lord thy God with all thy heart, and with all thy soul, and with all thy mind.

Matthew 22:37 KJV

The future belongs to those who see possibilities
before they become obvious.

—John Sculley

Now listen, you who say, "Today or tomorrow we will go to this or that city, spend a year there, carry on business and make money." Why, you do not even know what will happen tomorrow. What is your life? You are a mist that appears for a little while and then vanishes. Instead, you ought to say, "If it is the Lord's will, we will live and do this or that."

James 4:13–15

Know the true value of time; snatch, seize, and enjoy every
moment of it. No idleness, no laziness, no procrastination:
never put off till tomorrow what you can do today.

—*Lord Chesterfield*

Don't waste your time on useless work, mere busywork, the barren pursuits
of darkness. Expose these things for the sham they are.

Ephesians 5:11 MSG

No person has the right to rain on your dreams.

—*Marian Wright Edelman*

I can do all things through Christ who strengthens me.

Philippians 4:13 NKJV

We have a God who delights in impossibilities.

—Andrew Murray

Jesus said to them, "With people this is impossible, but with God all things are possible."

Matthew 19:26 NASB

Peace cannot be achieved through violence, it can only be attained through understanding.

—*Ralph Waldo Emerson*

Blessed are the peacemakers, for they will be called children of God.

Matthew 5:9

Obedience is an act of faith; disobedience is the result of unbelief.

—Edwin Louis Cole

As obedient children, do not be conformed to the passions of your former ignorance.

1 Peter 1:14, ESV

Snuggle in God's arms. When you are hurting, when you feel lonely, left out, let Him cradle you, comfort you, reassure you of His all-sufficient power and love.

—Kay Arthur

Let, I pray, Your merciful kindness be for my comfort.

Psalm 119:76 NKJV

You can give without loving, but you cannot love without giving.

—Amy Carmichael

It is more blessed to give than to receive.

Acts 20:35

At the height of laughter, the universe is flung into
a kaleidoscope of new possibilities.

—*Jean Houston*

He will yet fill your mouth with laughter and your lips with shouts of joy.

Job 8:21

Luck is a matter of preparation meeting opportunity.

—Oprah Winfrey

Make the most of every opportunity.

Colossians 4:5

We never test the resources of God until we attempt the impossible.

—*F. B. Meyer*

Faith is confidence in what we hope for and assurance about what we do not see.

Hebrews 11:1

To believe in God is to know that all the rules will be fair, and that there will be wonderful surprises!

—*Corita Kent*

God is not unjust; he will not forget your work and the love you have shown.

Hebrews 6:10

Problems are not stop signs, they are guidelines.

—*Robert H. Schuller*

When the way is rough, your patience has a chance to grow. So let it grow, and don't try to squirm out of your problems.

James 1:3–4 TLB

When you discipline yourself to do the things you need to do when you need to do them, the day will come when you can do the things you want to do when you want to do them.

—*Zig Ziglar*

Keep the charge of the LORD your God, walking in his ways and keeping his statutes, his commandments, his rules, and his testimonies, as it is written in the Law of Moses, that you may prosper in all that you do and wherever you turn.

1 Kings 2:3 ESV

A good head and a good heart are always a formidable combination.

—*Nelson Mandela*

Wisdom will enter your heart, and knowledge will fill you with joy.

Proverbs 2:10 NLT

The most valuable possession you can own is an open heart. The most powerful weapon you can be is an instrument of peace.

—*Carlos Santana*

I am leaving you with a gift—peace of mind and heart! And the peace I give isn't fragile like the peace the world gives. So don't be troubled or afraid.

John 14:27 TLB

If you're trying to achieve, there will be roadblocks. I've had them; everybody has had them. But obstacles don't have to stop you. If you run into a wall, don't turn around and give up. Figure out how to climb it, go through it, or work around it.

—*Michael Jordan*

Let us throw off everything that hinders and the sin that so easily entangles. And let us run with perseverance the race marked out for us.

Hebrews 12:1

Always do right. This will gratify some people, and astonish the rest.

—*Mark Twain*

This is a trustworthy saying, and I want you to insist on these teachings so that all who trust in God will devote themselves to doing good. These teachings are good and beneficial for everyone.

Titus 3:8 NLT

All life demands struggle. Those who have everything given to them become lazy, selfish, and insensitive to the real values of life. The very striving and hard work that we so constantly try to avoid is the major building block in the person we are today.

—*Pope Paul VI*

Give me neither poverty nor riches, but give me only my daily bread. Otherwise, I may have too much and disown you and say, "Who is the Lord?" Or I may become poor and steal, and so dishonor the name of my God.

Proverbs 30:8–9

It's not hard to make decisions when you know what your values are.

—*Roy Disney*

Daniel purposed in his heart that he would not defile himself.

Daniel 1:8 KJV

I would rather fail in the cause that someday will triumph
than triumph in a cause that someday will fail.

—*Woodrow Wilson*

Thanks be to God who always leads us in triumph in Christ.

2 Corinthians 2:14 NKJV

There is only one secure foundation: a genuine, deep relationship with Jesus Christ, which will carry you through any and all turmoil. No matter what storms are raging all around, you'll stand firm if you stand on His love.

—Charles Stanley

Christ's love compels us, because we are convinced that one died for all.

2 Corinthians 5:14

My faith isn't in the idea that I'm more moral than anybody else. My faith is in the idea that God and His love are greater than whatever sins any of us commit.

—*Rich Mullins*

I sought the LORD, and he answered me; he delivered me from all my fears.

Psalm 34:4

A true friend never gets in your way unless you happen to be going down.

—Arnold Glasow

If one falls, the other pulls him up; but if a man falls when he is alone, he's in trouble.

Ecclesiastes 4:10 TLB

Obedience to the call of Christ nearly always costs everything to two people: the one who is called, and the one who loves that one.

—Oswald Chambers

If you will indeed obey My voice and keep My covenant, then you shall be a special treasure to Me above all people; for all the earth is Mine.

Exodus 19:5 NKJV

I am determined to be cheerful and happy in
whatever situation I may find myself.

—*Martha Washington*

A cheerful disposition is good for your health; gloom and doom leave you bone-tired.

Proverbs 17:22 MSG

Whatever you dislike in another person, take care to correct in yourself.

—*Thomas Sprat*

Why do you look at the speck of sawdust in your brother's eye and pay no attention to the plank in your own eye?

Matthew 7:3

I count him braver who overcomes his desires than him who conquers his enemies; for the hardest victory is the victory over self.

—Aristotle

God has not given us a spirit of fear and timidity, but of power, love, and self-discipline.

2 Timothy 1:7 NLT

Trust in yourself and you are doomed to disappointment; ... but trust in God, and you are never to be confounded in time or eternity.

—*Dwight L. Moody*

Trust in the LORD with all your heart and lean not on your own understanding.

Proverbs 3:5

A knowledge of the Bible without a college course is more valuable than a college course without the Bible.

—William Lyon Phelps

All scripture is given by inspiration of God, and is profitable for doctrine, for reproof, for correction, for instruction in righteousness: That the man of God may be perfect, thoroughly furnished unto all good works.

2 Timothy 3:16–17 KJV

Never be afraid to trust an unknown future to a known God.

—*Corrie ten Boom*

I will turn the darkness into light before them and make the rough places smooth.

Isaiah 42:16

Success consists of getting up just one more time than you fall.

—*Oliver Goldsmith*

The righteous falls seven times and rises again, but the wicked stumble in times of calamity.

Proverbs 24:16 ESV

You are only what you are when no one is looking.

—*Robert C. Edwards*

Not by way of eyeservice, as men-pleasers, but as slaves of Christ, doing the will of God from the heart.

Ephesians 6:6 NASB

God gave us the gift of life; it is up to us to give ourselves the gift of living well.

—Voltaire

I have come that they may have life, and have it to the full.

John 10:10

Little minds are tamed and subdued by misfortune;
but great minds rise above it.

—Washington Irving

Consider it pure joy, my brothers and sisters, whenever you face trials of many kinds.

James 1:2

Perseverance is a great element of success. If you only knock long enough and loud enough at the gate, you are sure to wake up somebody.

—*Henry Wadsworth Longfellow*

Jesus told his disciples a story to illustrate their need for constant prayer and to show them that they must keep praying until the answer comes.

Luke 18:1

Do not seek to follow in the footsteps of the
men of old; seek what they sought.

—Matsuo Basho

I love everyone who loves me, and I will be found by all who honestly search.

Proverbs 8:17 CEV

One of Life's great rules is this: The more you give, the more you get.

—William H. Danforth

The generous will prosper; those who refresh others will themselves be refreshed.

Proverbs 11:25 NLT

To trust in Him when no need is pressing, when things seem going right of themselves, may be harder than when things seem going wrong.

—*George MacDonald*

Blessed is the one who trusts in the Lord.

Psalm 40:4

Shoot for the moon. Even if you miss, you'll land among the stars.

—*Les Brown*

Be strengthened (perfected, completed, made what you ought to be).

2 Corinthians 13:11 AMP

God is God. Because He is God, He is worthy of my trust and obedience. I will find rest nowhere but in His holy will, a will that is unspeakably beyond my largest notions of what He is up to.

—*Elisabeth Elliot*

It is better to take refuge in the Lord than to trust in humans.

Psalm 118:8

I am only one, but still I am one. I cannot do everything, but still I can do something.... I will not refuse to do the something that I can do.

—*Edward Everett Hale*

Under [Christ's] direction the whole body is fitted together perfectly, and each part in its own special way helps the other parts.

Ephesians 4:16 TLB

Anything I've ever done that ultimately was worthwhile initially scared me to death.

—*Betty Bender*

When I am afraid, I put my trust in you. In God, whose word I praise—in God I trust and am not afraid. What can mere mortals do to me?

Psalm 56:3–4

Never, never, never give up.

—*Winston Churchill*

As for you, brothers, do not grow weary in doing good.

2 Thessalonians 3:13 ESV

No matter what a man's past may have been, his future is spotless.

—John R. Rice

As far as the east is from the west, so far has he removed our transgressions from us.

Psalm 103:12

I have learned to live each day as it comes and not to borrow trouble by dreading tomorrow. It is the dark menace of the future that makes cowards of us all.

—*Dorothy Dix*

He will order his angels to protect you wherever you go.

Psalm 91:11 NLT

Remember not only to say the right thing in the right place, but far more difficult still, to leave unsaid the wrong thing at the tempting moment.

—*Benjamin Franklin*

Careful words make for a careful life; careless talk may ruin everything.

Proverbs 13:3 MSG

I think the one lesson I have learned is that there
is no substitute for paying attention.

—*Diane Sawyer*

We must pay more careful attention, therefore, to what we have heard, so that we do not drift away.

Hebrews 2:1

Perfection is not attainable, but if we chase perfection we can catch excellence.

—*Vince Lombardi*

Daniel was preferred above the presidents and princes, because an excellent spirit was in him.

Daniel 6:3 KJV

When we long for life without difficulties, remind us that oaks grow strong in contrary winds and diamonds are made under pressure.

—Peter Marshall

You must learn to endure everything, so that you will be completely mature and not lacking in anything.

James 1:4 CEV

The happiest people don't necessarily have the best of everything. They just make the best of everything.

—Author unknown

I have learned the secret of being content in any and every situation.

Philippians 4:12

Blessed is the man who finds out which way God is moving
and then gets going in the same direction.

—*Vance Havner*

Whether you turn to the right or to the left, your ears will hear a voice behind you, saying, "This is the way; walk in it."

Isaiah 30:21

Nothing is ever lost by courtesy.... It pleases him who gives and him who receives, and thus, like mercy, it is twice blessed.

—Erastus Wiman

While we have opportunity, let us do good to all people.

Galatians 6:10 NASB

Here's the key to success and the key to failure:
we become what we think about.

—Earl Nightingale

Whatever is true, whatever is noble, whatever is right, whatever is pure, whatever is lovely, whatever is admirable—if anything is excellent or praiseworthy—think about such things.

Philippians 4:8

Legalism says God will love us if we change. The gospel says God will change us because He loves us.

—*Tullian Tchividjian*

Being confident of this, that he who began a good work in you will carry it on to completion until the day of Christ Jesus.

Philippians 1:6

Though we are incomplete, God loves us completely. Though we are imperfect, He loves us perfectly. Though we may feel lost and without compass, God's love encompasses us completely.... He loves every one of us, even those who are flawed, rejected, awkward, sorrowful, or broken.

—*Dieter F. Uchtdorf*

I am convinced that neither death nor life, neither angels nor demons, neither the present nor the future, nor any powers, neither height nor depth, nor anything else in all creation, will be able to separate us from the love of God that is in Christ Jesus our Lord.

Romans 8:38–39

Sainthood lies in the habit of referring the smallest actions to God.

—*C. S. Lewis*

Therefore I tell you, do not be anxious about your life, what you will eat or what you will drink, nor about your body, what you will put on. Is not life more than food, and the body more than clothing? Look at the birds of the air: they neither sow nor reap nor gather into barns, and yet your heavenly Father feeds them. Are you not of more value than they?

Matthew 6:25–26 ESV

I learned that courage was not the absence of fear, but the triumph over it. The brave man is not he who does not feel afraid, but he who conquers that fear.

—*Nelson Mandela*

Have not I commanded you? Be strong, vigorous, and very courageous. Be not afraid, neither be dismayed, for the Lord your God is with you wherever you go.

Joshua 1:9 AMP

You may be disappointed if you fail, but you are doomed if you don't try.

—Beverly Sills

A sluggard's appetite is never filled, but the desires of the diligent are fully satisfied.

Proverbs 13:4

It's a good thing to have all the props pulled out from under us occasionally. It gives us some sense of what is rock under our feet, and what is sand.

—Madeleine L'Engle

He is the Rock, his works are perfect, and all his ways are just. A faithful God who does no wrong, upright and just is he.

Deuteronomy 32:4

Real prayer comes not from gritting our teeth but from falling in love.

—*Richard Foster*

By day the LORD directs his love, at night his song is with me—a prayer to the God of my life.

Psalm 42:8

Carve your name on hearts and not on marble.

—*Charles H. Spurgeon*

The only letter I need is you yourselves! ... They can see that you are a letter from Christ, written by us.... Not one carved on stone, but in human hearts.

2 Corinthians 3:2–3 TLB

It is impossible for that man to despair who remembers that his Helper is omnipotent.

—*Jeremy Taylor*

I will lift up my eyes to the mountains; from where shall my help come? My help comes from the LORD, who made heaven and earth.

Psalm 121:1–2 NASB

The world belongs to the man who is wise enough to change his mind in the presence of facts.

—*Roy L. Smith*

The one who heeds correction gains understanding.

Proverbs 15:32

Where fear is present, wisdom cannot be.

—*Lucius C. Lactantius*

The LORD is my light and my salvation—whom shall I fear?

Psalm 27:1

The world is governed more by appearance than realities.

—*Daniel Webster*

These are a shadow of the things that were to come; the reality, however, is found in Christ.

Colossians 2:17

Never despair; but if you do, work on in despair.

—*Edmund Burke*

As for you, be strong and do not give up, for your work will be rewarded.

2 Chronicles 15:7

Most of the things worth doing in the world had been declared impossible before they were done.

—*Louis D. Brandeis*

Nothing will be impossible with God.

Luke 1:37 ESV

When you are laboring for others, let it be with
the same zeal as if it were for yourself.

—*Confucius*

Put yourself aside, and help others get ahead. Don't be obsessed with getting your own advantage. Forget yourselves long enough to lend a helping hand.

Philippians 2:4 MSG

The most important single ingredient in the formula of success is knowing how to get along with people.

—*Theodore Roosevelt*

See that no one pays back evil for evil, but always try to do good to each other and to everyone else.

1 Thessalonians 5:15 TLB

Life must be understood backwards. But ... It must be lived forwards.

—Søren Kierkegaard

This is what the LORD says—your Redeemer, the Holy One of Israel: "I am the LORD your God, who teaches you what is best for you, who directs you in the way you should go."

Isaiah 48:17

Success is never final; failure is never fatal. It is courage that counts.

—Author unknown

Be of good courage, and he shall strengthen your heart, all ye that hope in the Lord.

Psalm 31:24 KJV

To love what you do and feel that it matters—
how could anything be more fun?

—Katharine Graham

My heart rejoiced in all my labour.

Ecclesiastes 2:10 KJV

Every calling is great when greatly pursued.

—*Oliver Wendell Holmes*

I press toward the mark for the prize of the high calling of God in Christ Jesus.

Philippians 3:14 KJV

When you were born, you cried and the world rejoiced. Live your life
in such a way that when you die, the world cries and you rejoice.

—Indian proverb

To me, living means living for Christ, and dying is even better.

Philippians 1:21 NLT

The secret of success is to do the common things uncommonly well.

—John D. Rockefeller Jr.

Do you see a man who excels in his work? He will stand before kings; he will not stand before unknown men.

Proverbs 22:29 NKJV

The cheerful man will do more in the same time, will do it better, will preserve it longer, than the sad or sullen.

—*Thomas Carlyle*

When a man is gloomy, everything seems to go wrong; when he is cheerful, everything seems right!

Proverbs 15:15 TLB

Only passions, great passions, can elevate the soul to great things.

—*Denis Diderot*

Fervent in spirit; serving the Lord.

Romans 12:11 KJV

The greater part of our happiness or misery depends
on our disposition and not our circumstances.

—*Martha Washington*

Keep your lives free from the love of money and be content with what you have, because God has said, "Never will I leave you; never will I forsake you."

Hebrews 13:5

Don't be discouraged; everyone who got where he is, started where he was.

—*John C. Maxwell*

Though your beginning was insignificant, yet your end will increase greatly.

Job 8:7 NASB

Prayer is an invisible tool which is wielded in a visible world.

—Leo Tolstoy

The weapons of our warfare are not carnal, but mighty through God to the pulling down of strong holds.

2 Corinthians 10:4 KJV

Perseverance is the hard work you do after you get tired of doing the hard work you already did.

—Newt Gingrich

Let us not become weary in doing good, for at the proper time we will reap a harvest if we do not give up.

Galatians 6:9

Destiny is no matter of chance: it is a matter of choice. It is not a thing to be waited for, it is a thing to be achieved.

—*William Jennings Bryan*

Whatever God has promised gets stamped with the Yes of Jesus.

2 Corinthians 1:20 MSG

It is amidst great perils we see brave hearts.

—*Jean-François Regnard*

I'm up again—rested, tall and steady, fearless before the enemy mobs coming at me from all sides.

Psalm 3:6 MSG

An error doesn't become a mistake until you refuse to correct it.

—*Orlando A. Battista*

Whoever heeds discipline shows the way to life, but whoever ignores correction leads others astray.

Proverbs 10:17

Hatred paralyzes life; love releases it. Hatred confuses life; love harmonizes it. Hatred darkens life; love illuminates it.

—*Martin Luther King Jr.*

If you are always biting and devouring one another, watch out! Beware of destroying one another.

Galatians 5:15 NLT

When you flee temptation, don't leave a forwarding address.

—Author unknown

Flee from youthful lusts and pursue righteousness ... with those who call on the Lord from a pure heart.

2 Timothy 2:22 NASB

We live in deeds, not years; in thoughts, not breaths....
We should count time by heart-throbs. He most lives
who thinks most, feels the noblest, acts the best.

—Philip James Bailey

"In him we live and move and have our being." As some of your own poets have said, "We are his offspring."

Acts 17:28

We need to discover all over again that worship is natural to the Christian, as it was to the godly Israelites who wrote the psalms, and that the habit of celebrating the greatness and graciousness of God yields an endless flow of thankfulness, joy, and zeal.

—*J. I. Packer*

The light in the eyes [of him whose heart is joyful] rejoices the hearts of others.

Proverbs 15:30 AMP

Children who bring honor to their parents reap blessings from their God.

—Author unknown

Honor your father and your mother, so that you may live long in the land the LORD our God is giving you.

Exodus 20:12

Laughter is the sun that drives winter from the human face.

—*Victor Hugo*

A merry heart maketh a cheerful countenance.

Proverbs 15:13 KJV

A good reputation is more valuable than money.

—*Publilius Syrus*

A good name is rather to be chosen than great riches.

Proverbs 22:1 KJV

Strive not to be a success, but rather to be of value.

—*Albert Einstein*

Am I now trying to win the approval of human beings, or of God?

Galatians 1:10

The Bible has a word to describe "safe" sex: It's called marriage.

—*Gary Smalley & John Trent*

Honor marriage, and guard the sacredness of sexual intimacy between wife and husband. God draws a firm line against casual and illicit sex.

Hebrews 13:4 MSG

Every charitable act is a stepping stone toward heaven.

—*Henry Ward Beecher*

Store your treasures in heaven, where moths and rust cannot destroy, and thieves do not break in and steal.

Matthew 6:20 NLT

Never be in a hurry; do everything quietly and in a calm spirit. Do not lose your inner peace for anything whatsoever, even if your whole world seems upset.

—*Saint Francis de Sales*

A hot-tempered person stirs up conflict, but the one who is patient calms a quarrel.

Proverbs 15:18

God has wisely kept us in the dark concerning future events, and reserved to himself the knowledge of them … that he may train us up in a dependence upon himself, and a continued readiness for every event.

—*Matthew Henry*

The vision is yet for an appointed time … It will surely come, it will not tarry.

Habakkuk 2:3 KJV

The mind grows by what it feeds on.

—*J. G. Holland*

The mind governed by the Spirit is life and peace.

Romans 8:6

All our dreams can come true, if we have the courage to pursue them.

—*Walt Disney*

Be strong and courageous. Do not be afraid or terrified because of them, for the Lord your God goes with you; he will never leave you nor forsake you.

Deuteronomy 31:6

Vision is the world's most desperate need. There are no hopeless situations, only people who think hopelessly.

—*Winifred Newman*

Where there is no vision, the people perish.

Proverbs 29:18 KJV

Once a word has been allowed to escape, it cannot be recalled.

—Horace

Do not let any unwholesome talk come out of your mouths, but only what is helpful for building others up according to their needs, that it may benefit those who listen.

Ephesians 4:29

It often happens that those of whom we speak
least on earth are best known in heaven.

—*Nicolas Caussin*

You are the ones chosen by God, chosen for the high calling of priestly work, chosen to be a holy people, God's instruments to do his work and speak out for him.

1 Peter 2:9 MSG

Motivation is when your dreams put on work clothes.

—*Benjamin Franklin*

From the fruit of their lips people are filled with good things, and the work of their hands brings them reward.

Proverbs 12:14

A good listener is not only popular everywhere, but after a while he gets to know something.

—*Wilson Mizner*

The ear that hears the rebukes of life will abide among the wise.

Proverbs 15:31 NKJV

The capacity to care ... gives life its deepest meaning and significance.

—Pablo Casals

Bear one another's burdens, and thereby fulfill the law of Christ.

Galatians 6:2 NASB

The only way to have a friend is to be one.

—*Ralph Waldo Emerson*

A man that hath friends must [show] himself friendly.

Proverbs 18:24 KJV

It is very presumptuous in me to wish to choose my path, because I cannot tell which path is best for me. I must leave it to the Lord, Who knows me, to lead me by the path which is best for me, so that in all things His will may be done.

—*Teresa of Avila*

In peace I will lie down and sleep, for you alone, O Lord, will keep me safe.

Psalm 4:8 NLT

The future belongs to those who believe in the beauty of their dreams.

—*Eleanor Roosevelt*

Anything is possible if you have faith.

Mark 9:23 TLB

God takes life's pieces and gives us unbroken peace.

—*W. D. Gough*

The peace of God, which surpasses all understanding, will guard your hearts and minds through Christ Jesus.

Philippians 4:7 NKJV

Jumping to conclusions is not half as good an exercise as digging for facts.

—Author unknown

Do your best to present yourself to God as one approved, a workman who does not need to be ashamed and who correctly handles the word of truth.

2 Timothy 2:15

He who created us without our help will not save us without our consent.

—*St. Augustine*

If you declare with your mouth, "Jesus is Lord," and believe in your heart that God raised him from the dead, you will be saved.

Romans 10:9

You can accomplish more in one hour with God
than one lifetime without Him.

—Author unknown

Your right hand sustains me; your help has made me great.

Psalm 18:35

To be a Christian means to forgive the inexcusable
because God has forgiven the inexcusable in you.

—*C. S. Lewis*

When you are praying, first forgive anyone you are holding a grudge against, so that your Father in heaven will forgive your sins, too.

Mark 11:25 NLT

God tests and proves us by the common occurrences of life. It is the little things which reveal the chapters of the heart.

—*Ellen G. White*

Examine yourselves to see whether you are in the faith; test yourselves.

2 Corinthians 13:5

Within your heart
Keep one still, secret spot
Where dreams may go,
And, sheltered so,
May thrive and grow.

—Louise Driscoll

Above all else, guard your heart, for everything you do flows from it.

Proverbs 4:23

Family is not an important thing. It's everything.

—Michael J. Fox

You should be like one big happy family ... loving one another with tender hearts and humble minds.

1 Peter 3:8 TLB

Patience and diligence, like faith, remove mountains.

—William Penn

Sloth makes you poor; diligence brings wealth.

Proverbs 10:4 MSG

Many receive advice, only the wise profit by it.

—Publilius Syrus

Where there is strife, there is pride, but wisdom is found in those who take advice.

Proverbs 13:10

Opportunities are seldom labeled.

—John A. Shedd

Ask and it will be given to you; seek and you will find; knock and the door will be opened to you.

Luke 11:9

Unless you try to do something beyond what you have
already mastered, you will never grow.

—Ralph Waldo Emerson

Brethren, I do not regard myself as having laid hold of it yet; but one thing I do: forgetting what lies behind and reaching forward to what lies ahead, I press on toward the goal for the prize of the upward call of God in Christ Jesus.

Philippians 3:13–14, NASB

Before you borrow money from a friend, decide which you need more.

—Author unknown

If anyone borrows an animal from their neighbor and it is injured or dies while the owner is not present, they must make restitution.

Exodus 22:14

Never fear shadows. They simply mean there's
a light shining somewhere nearby.

—Ruth E. Renkel

Yea, though I walk through the valley of the shadow of death, I will fear no evil: for thou art with me.

Psalm 23:4 KJV

Let us not say, Every man is the architect of his own fortune; but let us say, Every man is the architect of his own character.

—George Dana Boardman

I will defend my integrity until I die. I will maintain my innocence without wavering. My conscience is clear for as long as I live.

Job 27:5–6 NLT

Obstacles are those frightful things you see when you take your eyes off your goal.

—*Henry Ford*

We know that in all things God works for the good of those who love him, who have been called according to his purpose.

Romans 8:28

The Bible knows nothing of a hierarchy of labor. No work is degrading. If it ought to be done, then it is good work.

—*Author unknown*

Whatever you do, work at it with all your heart, as working for the Lord, not for human masters.

Colossians 3:23

'Tis better to be alone than in bad company.

—George Washington

Do not be misled: "Bad company corrupts good character."

1 Corinthians 15:33

I like the dreams of the future better than the history of the past.

—*Thomas Jefferson*

Forget about what's happened; don't keep going over old history. Be alert, be present. I'm about to do something brand-new. It's bursting out! Don't you see it?

Isaiah 43:18–19 MSG

You can lead a boy to college, but you cannot make him think.

—*Elbert Hubbard*

It is senseless to pay tuition to educate a rebel who has no heart for truth.

Proverbs 17:16 TLB

Unless we form the habit of going to the Bible in bright moments as well as in trouble, we cannot fully respond to its consolations because we lack equilibrium between light and darkness.

—*Helen Keller*

No discipline is enjoyable while it is happening—it's painful! But afterward there will be a peaceful harvest of right living for those who are trained in this way.

Hebrews 12:11 NLT

God never put anyone in a place too small to grow in.

—*Henrietta Mears*

Give thanks in all circumstances, for this is God's will for you in Christ Jesus.

1 Thessalonians 5:18

Maturity: Be able to stick with a job until it is finished. Be able to bear an injustice without having to get even. Be able to carry money without spending it. Do your duty without being supervised.

—Ann Landers

When I was a child, I spoke as a child, I understood as a child, I thought as a child; but when I became a man, I put away childish things.

1 Corinthians 13:11 NKJV

You must have long-range goals to keep you from
being frustrated by short-range failures.

—*Charles C. Noble*

[Let us fix] our eyes on Jesus, the pioneer and perfecter of faith. For the joy set before him he endured the cross, scorning its shame, and sat down at the right hand of the throne of God.

Hebrews 12:2

Many men have too much willpower. It's won't power they lack.

—Author unknown

A man without self-control is as defenseless as a city with broken-down walls.

Proverbs 25:28 TLB

Politeness goes very far, yet it costs nothing.

—*Samuel Smiles*

Those who are kind benefit themselves.

Proverbs 11:17

Keep your fears to yourself, but share your inspiration with others.

—*Robert Louis Stevenson*

Honor Christ and let him be the Lord of your life. Always be ready to give an answer when someone asks you about your hope.

1 Peter 3:15 CEV

Life is like a coin. You can spend it any way you wish, but you only spend it once.

—*Lillian Dickson*

It is appointed unto men once to die, but after this the judgment.

Hebrews 9:27 KJV

Truth, like surgery, may hurt, but it cures.

—*Han Suyin*

Speaking the truth in love, we will grow to become in every respect the mature body of him who is the head, that is, Christ.

Ephesians 4:15

Don't count on your education to make you wise.

—*Author unknown*

Those who trust in themselves are fools, but those who walk in wisdom are kept safe.

Proverbs 28:26

Most of the verses written about praise in God's Word were voiced by people who were faced with crushing heartaches, injustice, treachery, slander, and scores of other difficult situations.

—*Joni Eareckson Tada*

David sang to the LORD ... when the LORD delivered him from the hand of all his enemies ... He said: "The LORD is my rock, my fortress and my deliverer."

2 Samuel 22:1–2

We too often love things and use people when we should be using things and loving people.

—*Reuel Howe*

Love each other with genuine affection, and take delight in honoring each other.

Romans 12:10 NLT

You can't test courage cautiously.

—*Annie Dillard*

So do not fear, for I am with you; do not be dismayed, for I am your God. I will strengthen you and help you; I will uphold you with my righteous right hand.

Isaiah 41:10

I believe that God is managing affairs and that He doesn't need any advice from me. With God in charge, I believe everything will work out for the best in the end. So what is there to worry about?

—*Henry Ford*

Search me, God, and know my heart; test me and know my anxious thoughts.

Psalm 139:23

I have also decided to stick with love.... Hate is too great a burden to bear.

—*Martin Luther King Jr.*

Do everything in love.

1 Corinthians 16:14

To believe in something, and not to live it, is dishonest.

—*Mahatma Gandhi*

If we live by the Spirit, let us also walk by the Spirit.

Galatians 5:25 NASB

Some debts are fun when you are acquiring them, but
none are fun when you set about retiring them.

—Ogden Nash

Why do you spend money for what is not bread, and your wages for what does not satisfy? Listen carefully to Me, and eat what is good, and delight yourself in abundance.

Isaiah 55:2 NASB

In His will is our peace.

—*Dante Alighieri*

Great peace have those who love Your law, and nothing causes them to stumble.

Psalm 119:165 NKJV

Diligence is the mother of good fortune.

—*Cervantes*

The plans of the diligent lead to profit.

Proverbs 21:5

I am convinced that faith sometimes means knowing God can, whether or not He does.

—*Beth Moore*

The God we worship can save us from you and your flaming furnace. But even if he doesn't, we still won't worship your gods and the gold statue you have set up.

Daniel 3:17–18 CEV

Let your words be the genuine picture of your heart.

—*John Wesley*

My mouth shall speak wisdom, and the meditation of my heart shall give understanding.

Psalm 49:3 NKJV

Call on God, but row away from the rocks.

—*Indian proverb*

Wisdom and good judgment live together, for wisdom knows where to discover knowledge and understanding.

Proverbs 8:12 TLB

We need to pay more attention to how we treat people than to how they treat us.

—Joyce Meyer

Love others as well as you love yourself.

Mark 12:31 MSG

If one advances confidently in the direction of his dreams, and endeavors to live the life he has imagined, he will meet with a success unexpected.

—*Henry David Thoreau*

"I know the plans I have for you," declares the Lord, "plans to prosper you and not to harm you, plans to give you hope and a future.

Jeremiah 29:11

Unless otherwise noted, all Scripture quotations are taken from the Holy Bible, New International Version®, NIV®. Copyright © 1973, 2011 by Biblica, Inc.™ Used by permission of Zondervan. All rights reserved worldwide. www.zondervan.com.

Scripture quotations marked KJV are taken from the King James Version of the Bible. (Public Domain.)

Scripture quotations marked MSG are taken from *THE MESSAGE*. Copyright © by Eugene H. Peterson 1993, 2002. Used by permission of NavPress Publishing Group.

Scripture quotations marked NASB are taken from the New American Standard Bible®, Copyright © 1960, 1995 by The Lockman Foundation. Used by permission. (www.Lockman.org.)

Scripture quotations marked NKJV are taken from the New King James Version®. Copyright © 1982 by Thomas Nelson, Inc. Used by permission. All rights reserved.

Scripture quotations marked TLB are taken from The Living Bible, © 1971, Tyndale House Publishers, Wheaton, IL 60189. Used by permission.

Scripture quotations marked NLT are taken from the *Holy Bible*, New Living Translation, copyright © 1996, 2007 by Tyndale House Foundation. Used by permission of Tyndale House Publishers, Inc., Carol Stream, Illinois 60188. All rights reserved.

Scripture quotations marked CEV are taken from the Contemporary English Version © 1991, 1995 by American Bible Society. Used by permission.

Scripture quotations marked AMP are taken from the Amplified® Bible. Copyright © 1954, 1987 by The Lockman Foundation. Used by permission. (www.Lockman.org.)